THE G-CODE: BEHIND THE BARS

A HIP-HOP CONNOISSEUR'S GUIDE THROUGH CORPORATE AMERICA

LEMAR INGRAM

"NEVER COVER TO COVER
NOT YOUR BASIC
AVERAGE OR REGULAR
COVERED ON THE CORNERS.
SCAN. FOLLOW THE
FORMULA.
READ AND DIGEST PAUSE
AND DIGRESS. JOT YOUR
THOUGHTS TAKE NOTES.
DISCOVER THE G-CODE.
THE CONCEPT AIN'T COMPLEX.
PEEP THE CONTENT
IN CONTEXT.
1 CHAPTER AT A TIME.
REFLECT. . .
PAUSE

PROGRESS"

INSTRUCTIONS:

THIS MANUAL IS NOT MEANT TO BE READ COVER TO COVER.
THIS IS NOT A "REGULAR" BOOK PLEASE FOLLOW THE GUIDELINES BELOW.

STEP 1: Read the chapter.
Scan barcode to access audio book if you prefer
(Use site to access reference material)

STEP 2: Reflect on the individual chapter and utilize the journal
to capture your notes and thoughts

STEP 3: Move on to the next chapter (at your pace)

STEP 4: Review your journal entries upon completion of the book

STEP 5: Repeat as needed

CONTENTS

PREFACE

0 MY NAME IS MY NAME
1 GET YOUR BARS UP
2 BEING A GROUPIE IS NOT A FLEX
3 MAKE IT LOOK EFFORTLESS
4 LET THEM USE YOU
5 NAVIGATING THE HIGHLANDS
6 THE SYNTHESIS OF ALL YOU KNOW
7 YOU SHOULDN'T HAVE TO SAY SORRY
8 CAN'T BE MAD AT ZEBRAS FOR HAVING STRIPES
9 READING AIN'T FUNDAMENTAL
10 FINNA BE CONSEQUENCES AND REPERCUSSIONS
11 MAMA AIN'T RAISE NO HOES
12 WHO BRUNG YOU AND WHO YOU BROUGHT

LAST WORDS

PREFACE

In an interview, a candidate looked directly into the camera and stated, "I want to be a billionaire". Strange response to a question regarding goals as an entry level salesperson. I asked if he had a degree, he defiantly responded no. When you think on it, more than ever, the cost of a college degree makes it unattainable for some, while others question its value and validity.
Does Elon Musk, Shawn Carter, Sean Combs any of the businessmen you respect have one?
He quoted an instagram post that stated bluntly, If X amount of people get a degree annually the value of your degree is depreciating.

That perspective was daunting, in my opinion supremely inaccurate. It triggered a series of observations and philosophical moments, maybe that was the provocateur's goal.

I looked at these billionaires and started analyzing what they had in common. Why were they able to achieve that level of success without a formal education?

My conclusion: education does not have to be formal. Socratic learning was the standard but not the only methodology. Like an apprenticeship, nurture can teach the skills one needs to be successful. Simply put in the right circumstances you have a head start.
This might explain billionaires that come from "good environments".

Some billionaires were not born into the ideal circumstances, how did they make it?

The billionaire goal is aspirational.

Taking a step back: What about a solid life, a six-figure salary, white picket fence and how many ever kids you want? If you did not need a college degree to be a billionaire, do you need one to be successful? Looking around the boardroom at my mentors, counterparts, and coworkers I realized nurture mattered but format doesn't. Lessons can be learned via positive or negative environments. All that matters is how you apply them. We've all heard it before a hustler could be an ideal CEO candidate. Problem is they know the lessons but not the corporate application. The hustlers apply the G-Code as demanded on the streets, brutal and unforgiving. Results from this methodology aren't sustainable or legal. That's what others have figured out. They cracked it, learn both the lesson and the application methodology, that's the key. This realization prompted the idea for this book and the original chapter: ***...I wrote me a manual***. As you explore this publication reflect on how you apply the code we know. As the children of hip hop some of us have lived it.

Some of us observed it.
Subliminally we all know it.
It's time we learn how to use it.

Let's explore the G-Code.

...I WROTE ME A MANUAL:

The trappings and threads are equal to what's trapped in your head.

Stature matters, your stats, and math, as important as degrees and pedigree.

Have the look, it's important.

Know the look when you get it, in that look, there's a message.

Speak up, look around, after you said it.

Look past where you're heading.

Keep your head in the game, at all times.

It's not the same rules, yet the same place.

BEHIND THE BARS!!

Same look, a different face.
Face it, sometimes you're worried.

Are they faking?

Take in the situation.

They're taking your creative,
with compensation, ownership is where the stake is.

What's at stake is your reputation.

Your name is made when rooks look, to see who made moves.

Pawns deliver jewels in hopes of elevation.

Checkmates based on the king,others die way before the game ends,
know your station.

Watch your affiliations,dance with who brought you
and know whom you came with.

Be smart enough to jump if the ship sinks,
don't abandon, there's a difference.

There's security in loyalty, the cut off is reciprocity.

Them with you, that's a "WE", so we'll make it.

THE CORPORATE COMMANDMENTS INSPIRED BY
THE NOTORIOUS B.I.G.'S, *10 CRACK COMMANDMENTS,*
1997

CHAPTER 0
MY NAME IS MY NAME

I always knew I wasn't meant to be a worker bee. I loved the idea of being paid to think. I fell in love with trading ideas for money instead of time. That's the proper way to say it, the reality is like most of my boys I liked fast money. **"Nine to Five is how you survive, I ain't trying to survive, I'm trying to live it to the limit and love it a lot"** (Jay Z).

My mother was an author, preacher, life coach and teacher, she valued education and impact over money. I'm thankful that "calling" was not hereditary. Make no mistake like most Trini women Dr. Corridon aka Doxy was an uncompromising G.

She fostered my love for the written word Shakespeare, Chaucer, and Rostand's character: Cyrano. She instilled an appreciation for oration in me that became the foundation of my path.

I came up during the golden age of rap. Biggie, JayZ, Nas, Kool G Rap, AZ, Guru, Smif-n-Wesson, these dudes molded my mind. I didn't listen to rap, I memorized it all bar for bar, intonation, and cadence. I'm a rap Stan and it became my religion. Most if not all my missteps were inspired by my dogmatic obedience to rap lyrics. School dropout.... never liked that shit from day one.

Nas spoke to my quiet rebellion against the standard.
I never wanted to fit in, my goal was to stick out.
I always prioritized merit over favor.
I had the makings of an entrepreneur
and somehow ended up in corporate America.

My ability to relate everything to rap lyrics allowed me to spot similarities and connections between worlds. Not just hip-hop culture and corporate culture but street life and office life. I call it being inside or outside. The rules of engagement aren't similar they are identical.

To the chagrin of my mentors, I carried myself in accordance with the culture I embodied. I had the suit on, but I walked with that bop Nas references in his song Represent. I was rough around the edges, but it was motivated by the desire to be unapologetically me. I wanted everyone to see who I was from fifty yards away. I didn't mind preconceived notions because I knew what I brought to the table. Underestimate me at your peril, bias was a blind spot I used to my advantage. Dave would always say they never see you coming. That's ironic when you consider the fact, I'm a six foot one, three hundred pound (+) black guy.

MY BRAND:

AUTHENTICITY.

MY MOTTO:

WHAT IT IS, IS MORE IMPORTANT THAN HOW IT LOOKS.

MY NAME:

LEMAR INGRAM

MY NAME
IS MY NAME

CHAPTER 1
GET YOUR BARS UP....

Cuz *the streets is a short stop you either slingin' crack rock or you got a wicked jump-shot* (Notorious B.I.G.). Why would you listen to such a pessimistic life perspective?

The music reinforces stereotypes and pushes a negative agenda.
So, make sure you listen to it. Hell make sure you memorize it.
Then learn how to do it, be a proficient spitter.
People underestimate the power of rote knowledge.
The value of public speaking and the awe created by an eloquent impromptu response. In the adult world it's *hippity-hop* foolishness but in the halls of academia its alliteration, iambic pentameter, and extemporaneous speech.

It's always the same beat; boom bap, ba-boom bap,
boom bap, ba-boom bap, (props if you read it on beat).
All of a sudden, every wanna be rapper perks up.
Then someone sets it off:

> See I'm the nicest,
>
> Shine the brightest,
>
> Super nova....

Some other kid builds up the courage to spit the rhyme he has been working on for a week. Trying to pass it off as a "freestyle". It doesn't matter if they can spit, what matters is they had the fortitude to try. To open themselves up to the oohs, ahhhs and ridicule of a critical audience which rivals any Russian gymnastic judge.

Here is what you learn from the **hippity-hop** music:

1. Public speaking is one of the biggest fears, by performing before a critical engaged audience you conquer the apprehension associated with public speaking.

2. Memorizing your rhymes, by practicing your lines you enhance your ability to intentionally retain large amounts of information.

3. Extemporaneous response aka freestyling, practicing this art form allows you to correlate subject matter quickly. Connecting the dots faster than your peers will always make you stand out.

4. Rhythmic speech and alliteration make you an interesting speaker. People will pay attention because of your way with words.

    This helps when doing presentations/training.

BUT WHAT IF I'M NOT THAT NICE?

The key is to try and to practice. You may not be the next DMX but what you will do is sharpen your sword (Wu- Tang Slang). Your competition would not have trained the way you did. They would not have put in the requisite time. It's easy to log 10,000 hours when you are having fun. What will be perceived as a natural flair for speaking and presentation is a skill that you developed throughout your adolescent years. They who control the narrative often determine the outcome.

Start rappin'

CHAPTER 2
BEING A GROUPIE IS NOT A FLEX.

What we don't do is yes-manning, over-talking, emulating and overly compromising. The code doesn't allow for groupies, fanboys, or cheerleaders. While that path may offer less resistance, in the end you won't recognize who you are.

YES MANNING:

We are all inspired by mentors and leaders, it is imperative that you know they don't need yes men. When you're "outside" you wouldn't consistently second everything anyone says, no matter who they are. You may nod in agreement or use your lack of rebuttal as an endorsement. It's ok to let words fall whoever catch it... catch it. Same rules apply.

OVER TALKING:

In an environment where politeness is often prioritized over efficiency it's easy to fall into the trap of talking too muckin fuch. "Outside" people will be quick to tell you shut up, contrarily within corporate America you simply won't be invited to the next meeting, especially if you don't add value.

The real question is why are you talking?
Do you have something to say?
Are you trying to impress someone?

Abraham Lincoln has been credited with the quote:

It's better to close your mouth and appear stupid than to open your mouth and remove all doubt. Talking impresses no one. Outside you let your work speak for you.

Same rules apply.

EMULATING:

You are on the team because you offer a unique perspective or skill set. Don't try to be the next gyal or guy. An original you beats a photocopy of them every time. When push comes to shove you keep the essential parts not the replicas. It's never been ok to replicate someone else's style. You can admire, they can inspire but you need to have an individual fingerprint. Often when assimilating into a new environment people attempt to replicate the conduct of those they perceive as powerful or dominant in the hierarchy. Boardroom or Biscayne fact is you have to be you. Same rules apply.

OVER COMPROMISING:

You'll find yourself in agreement at times, other times you'll be standing alone. Your rules are your rules. They may not be written down, but you know the tenets of you. One can adjust principles because of a change in belief but one should not be changing beliefs daily. If it doesn't work for you then it doesn't work for you. Don't go along to get along on things that you think are wrong. Behind closed doors voice your disagreement even if you continue the elected path. Knowing where you stand and understanding how you proceed is a testament to the maturity required to succeed, with respect. Inside or outside same rules apply.

Taking this path may be difficult but you'll owe no favors and more importantly your choices will be easier. At times, the progress will be slow, but the foundation will be strong. Jada said it best: I know I'm way better than them other dudes, but I'm stuck with what I'm stuck with cuz I don't duck sick.

Same rules.

CHAPTER 3
MAKE IT LOOK EFFORTLESS

Anyone who tells you it's easy to be successful is a liar. Inside or outside getting to the bag is not easy. The goal is not a one-time lick. The goal is consistency. To be consistently successful requires hard work, a solid foundation and vigilance.

I don't know how you define success. It could be a number, title, or lifestyle. Once you define your version of success the key is to have a plan, and effectively execute the plan while refining it. There is the plan to get there, the plan to stay there and the plan to increase the scope of your success. With that being said, what could B.I.G. possibly have meant when he said,

"climb the ladder to success escalator style"?

No matter how hard the journey it's your responsibility to make it look effortless. Operating under the guise of ease creates an aura of success that attracts the right people. Your superiors know you can handle pressure. Your peers know they can rely on you.
Your subordinates gain confidence from your perceived nonchalance. No matter how difficult, don't complain or lament publicly. It's not as simple as being quiet. Crafting the "escalator style" brand requires a bit of finesse.

BE NICE TO EVERYONE

If you watched New Jack City the scene where Nino hands out turkeys for the holidays brings the question, why? Why would he do that? Scoring points and getting credit for being nice matters.

A mentor of mine told me how you treat security and custodial services in a corporation is as important as how you treat the C suite level executives. Think about it, it's nice to be nice.

ORGANIZE YOUR DAY TO INCLUDE TIME TO SOCIALIZE

Why do the ones outside go to the club? Why do they ball out? You must be amongst the people. This concept holds true inside as well. You can't be so high up that you're above people. Your job is to be inspirational as well as aspirational. Be the person they all want to be like. Be the person everyone can talk to.

SCHEDULE TO COMPLETE EVERYTHING BEFORE IT'S DUE

Procrastination is the enemy of success. Structure and order will allow time for you to think and execute. More importantly it will give you time to refine. If you're in a rush to complete a task before deadline, will
it be your best work? Developing your vision is more about reflection than the work.

WORK WHEN EVERYONE ELSE IS ASLEEP

Work life balance is the mantra of the day. The reality is it's about priority. In the establishment phase, when you are building your foundation, you will work more than you have fun. Mike Jones laid it out simple and plain: **If you don't work you don't eat, if you don't grind you don't shine.** Put in the extra time initially.

So, you can truly enjoy the fruit of your labor later.
The key here is to be low key about the hours you put in. Let no one be able to tally your hours; not bosses, peers, or subordinates.

End result....it just comes easy to you (well at least it looks that way)

CHAPTER 4
LET THEM USE YOU

People often confuse being used with being useful. If one is being used or not is a matter of perspective. To be used is to be taken advantage of. Make no mistake if you provide a service without any reciprocity, you are being used. However, to be useful is to be of value and service. When one is useful relationships are forged, connections are made an exchange takes place. Tee, another mentor, said kiss ass 'til you can kick it. He does have a point, but that's not me. You can't be top dog if you aren't taught how to. Without mentors to give you the code how do you learn it? Simple: Let them use you. More precisely let them think they are using you. Even better said make yourself useful, a resource.

Identify two key people, the head of the organization and their second in command. Everyone wants to win over the big boss because they think it's strategic. That move is basic and lacks vision. You don't want to be one of many acolytes. You want to be "the" acolyte. The big boss is advised by the most trusted subordinate, the second in command.

Avail yourself to this person. To avail oneself is a simple task. Identify the needs:

- What's important to them?
- What's their biggest obstacle?
    - How can you make their job easier?

Figure these things out and resolve them. If you don't know how to provide the service they need, learn it.

If it requires you take a class or a course, do it.

Do it before they ask and be good at it.

Why would you do this? The initial benefit is obvious, the second in command has the ear of the boss. Your service to this individual will result in them being your biggest advocate. Secondarily as the second in command becomes reliant on you, they will also begin to teach you. Here is where your education takes place. This is how you are nurtured. Pay attention to how they act, what they say, your teachable moments will not come with an announcement. Learn by being present and attentive. In time you may even become a surrogate for them. While this apprentice relationship evolves make sure your skillset does as well. You are only useful if you can provide the services needed by the second in command.

While most people do not consider an education proper compensation, elevation is also a derivative of this strategy. As positions open within the organization your newfound advocate will position you to be successful. Your advocate does not owe you they have taught you and that is more than enough. The opportunities you are positioned for are yours to maximize. Eventually the second in command will become the new boss, in this organization or another. The work you put in will be rewarding but you'll also be rewarded.

CHAPTER 5
NAVIGATING THE HIGHLANDS

The movie is called Highlander, directed by Russell Mulcahy (1986). The exact quote is: **There can be only one.** This premise was the impetus the immortals lived by. Ultimately only one could hold the key position. They were all capable and immortal. They could divide the earth and flourish forever, instead they opted for mutual destruction.

This philosophy has permeated all aspects of society. It's a belief system simultaneously grounded in scarcity and greed. The highlanders' mindset has dictated how we operate both inside and outside.

So why does this matter to you? Peep game as you begin on your path to success the culture you enter may be driven by highlanders. Be attentive to mentors who are not advocates, organizations that claim diversity but accomplish it via a "check the box" mentality as well as a lack of an organizational continuity plan.

Listen for red flags and warning signs from credible peers:

- I'm the only "(insert adjective)" in the room
- They only promote after someone leaves
- Tenure is more important than talent

The way we perceive the world dictates our approach to life. If we see opportunities as scarce, we operate with a sense of desperate urgency and fear.

We shift focus from maximizing opportunities to hoarding opportunities.

An alternate perspective would be, we can create opportunities.
This perspective relieves panic. We can materialize our vision via analysis and execution.

This isn't a "secret" mindset. It's a strategic approach to the game. Forget what's presented to you. Do not worry about the operations' organizational chart. Honestly, even their philosophy of doing business is irrelevant. **There is no spoon** (Matrix reference). Instead focus on the goals of the business and what you can do to facilitate them. Mentally construct scenarios that allow for the expansion of the business rather than operating within the confinement of the "norms".

Easier said than done...not really.

Key fact, you are an individual with a unique life journey.
All your experiences allow you to have a perspective that while not singular, is not common. If the culture is linear be creative.
If it's nontraditional explore the impact of structure.
Sometimes it's optimization other times innovation.

When you identify (create) the opportunity...execute.
While operating within a highlander culture how you execute is important. Take steps to document your efforts, these should include time stamps, emails and working docs that establish a project timeline. The goal here is to establish yourself as the driving force behind the project. In the highlands new initiatives are seldom met with excitement, expect to be disregarded and marginalized until there are proven results. Failure is an orphan and success have numerous parents round these parts. Work with at least two members of management (wouldn't hurt if they were rivals). This will assure the right eyes are aware of your efforts. Learning and doing is more important than credit, but recognition is important for progress. Through it all don't let this environment change who you are.

You're just passing through on your way to success.

HIM

18

CHAPTER 6
THE SYNTHESIS OF ALL YOU KNOW

Most people don't realize all they know. Even less utilize what they know. Life's experiences teach you. Some lessons are obvious others are so subtle, they change you and restructure your modus operandi unbeknownst to you. Point is you slicker than you think fam. This innate knowledge is more valuable than you think. The key is being able to access it at the right time. Start by taking mental inventory of what you know, if you prefer write it down. The practice of journaling helps you to reflect, itemize and organize your experiences. As you consciously expand your library of lessons and learnings you will notice patterns and solutions. How you apply these solutions will determine how successful you are. Some people take a very literal approach to problem solving. The person who is open to abstract, nonlinear thinking can craft solutions derived from unrelated experiences. A simple version of this is the individual who tears the house apart looking for a flathead screwdriver versus the person who uses a butter knife. Either way the problem is solved but the person who is efficient while being effective is more of an asset. Maybe you saw someone do it before, maybe a childhood obsession with puzzles gave you a better grasp of positive and negative space, whatever the reason the ability to reference that knowledge at the right moment is a difference maker.

Benny the Butcher said it best:

***When both hands full I ain't panic...
I juggle (solution).***

Theoretical examples don't always resonate so let's look
at a real-life case (true story):

• He went to SCAD to be an architect and realized they didn't
make the money he was looking for but thats how he learned about
Frank Lloyd Wright.

• FLW said Music and architecture blossom on the same stem....
• He loved rapping so why not try Sound Design as a major.
• That wasn't a major yet, so he started Video and Film.
• Later, he convinced the school to start a Sound Design major
• That lead him to freelancing at MTV.
• Somehow, he ends up at Home Depot working in flooring.
• Funny thing about that is he noticed how they trained employees.

The system they utilized allowed all employees to be cross trained on
demand.

• Later when he worked in Outbound Sales at Carnival Cruise Line.
They neededto train the staff on a new CRM (Opportunity)

The synthesis of all he knew:

• He had the confidence to convince a VP at CCL to let him implement
his solution an on-demand training video. Like the ones at Home Depot
(spit game strong ...chapter 1).

• He used his knowledge of college administration to get free
equipment and staff to shoot the training video.

• The film and video/ sound design experience helped with the
editing and creation of the on-demand training.

Outcome:

This was the first step of him becoming a director.

CHAPTER 7
YOU SHOULDN'T HAVE TO SAY SORRY

Temperamental I snap quick.... very touchy. My attitude is all f****d up and real shitty. Word to Prodigy you could be thoro or you could be smart. The choice is yours. The damage inflicted by misspeaking can ruin relationships before they start, or worse, destroy existing relationships.

When you're outside being moody isn't an issue if you can handle conflict. Inside, might doesn't make right and heart doesn't trump logic. Get out your feelings! No one is trying to play you or make you look stupid. Being completely honest, if they are, your response dictates the outcome. Outside a harsh emotional response is a sign of strength. Inside a calculated unwavering calm is the epitome of strength. React according to where you're standing. Most importantly, after you bark you normally must circle back and say sorry, inside.

People will create circumstances or say things that make you want to flip. Eyes are always going to be on you. You're the unique one, the one they are watching. Have your protocols and go to tactics that temper a harsh response. It may be "please give me a moment", "I'll be right with you", one that works. Don't transfer sentiment from situation A to situation B. Yes, they may have asked a silly question at the most inopportune time, but your reaction will dictate future interactions. The amount of time spent repairing relationships damaged from an off-color response or flippant comment made in a moment of frustration is significant.

People don't forget how you make them feel.
Especially if you make them feel inadequate, irrelevant, or stupid. Your job is to impact and influence the environment in a manner that is conducive to growth and advancement. Having to repurpose time to correct a moment with a single individual is damaging enough but the reputation of a hot head requires more repair. Your efforts should be focused on the prior not the latter.

Accidents will happen; **"you can make a couple mistakes just don't repeat it"** (38 Spesh). Focus on communicating the right way the first time. Nurture may have conditioned you otherwise so this skill will require practice. It only takes 21 days to develop a new habit and 365 days for it to become engrained.

22

ADDITIONALLY:

Don't speak on what you don't know.
Gossip isn't good no matter where you are standing
(inside or outside). Regardless of how you feel, If you can't
say it to their face.... don't.

If you're focused on your vision and accomplishing your
goals, where will you find the time to engage in mindless,
purposeless talk?

Don't stand too close to that type of activity.
If you weren't there your name can't be called.

The dog that carries a bone will bring one.
The last thing you need is a miscommunication
based on assumed participation in foolishness.
Then you have to be sorry for the misunderstanding?

Nah!

The goal is to make sure you don't have to say I'm sorry.

CHAPTER 8
CAN'T BE MAD AT ZEBRAS FOR HAVING STRIPES

People are always going to be who they are. If you're outside know that you're in an environment where survival is literally at stake. If you are inside your survival is still at stake but not mortally. This type of energy makes us cynical at best or withdrawn. Be open to the idea of good people while paying attention. Be analytically observant. Never get upset because people don't live up to your ideals. Expectations are not the root of disappointment; disappointment is the result of not heeding your intuition.

When Bishop laid claim to the gun in Juice it was obvious. His mentality was about short-term glory over sustained success. The consequences of his actions were always a distant second to his perceived glory. Why were we shocked when he shot Raheem? We wanted to believe that was his man, his road dog. The writing was always on the wall. Do you think it's different inside? When a peer values their progress over your future the play is the same. Competition exists inside and outside. We compete, recognition is the reward, the result is often success. During that journey character is always revealed. Who is the most sinister? Who is the purist? Who is vicious and purpose driven?

As you observe the behavior take note of what you see. Know your peer group as you know yourself. What drives them? How far they would go to win? Gauge the moral compass collectively as well as individually. This information will be valuable in the long run.

When you know who you are dealing with and what drives them predictive analysis should decrease the likelihood of you being surprised, disappointed, or hurt. Awareness of who and what you are dealing with helps you operate with an increased level of efficiency.
Trust people to be who they show you they are.
In a race the faster the horses are individually the faster the race. To achieve the most effective outcome they line up the faster horses next to each other. Occasionally there may be a contender that looks like a horse, struts like a horse but isn't fast. If your observant you'll notice stripes, that's a zebra. While a zebra may have purpose it's definitely not a racehorse. You can't line that animal up against horses and expect it to compete.
Understanding who you're working with allows you to allocate resources accordingly resulting in two key successes:

1. You get the most out of the situation
2. Your success metric is properly calibrated

Expecting a zebra to be a horse is as ludicrous as expecting it to be a tiger because it has stripes. Preconceived notions based on hope or a tainted perspective instead of the reality of objective assessment will always lead to frustration. Don't expect milk from bees, eggs from cows, don't try to drown fish and the last thing you want to be is mad at a zebra for having stripes.

CHAPTER 9
READING AIN'T FUNDAMENTAL

As you read this, I want you to be cognizant of a key fact: the world is changing. There was a time when the only way to access information was reading. If you couldn't or didn't read your chances for success were significantly diminished. This is why for a while some of us weren't even allowed to know how to read. Being cut off from information made us unaware of options. Cam said it best SDE: sports, drugs, and entertainment till the arraignment. If you subscribed to that mindset the destination was predetermined.

What changed? Access changed! Before you had to have access to the scrolls. The knowledge was "hidden" in books.
If you didn't have access, then you needed a library. The scope of your knowledge was based on the publications housed within your library. Sometimes it was outdated or incorrect and the only perspective you could have was the author's.
The internet, smart phone, social media, and podcasts have made information easily accessible.

With 85% of us having smartphones access to information is limitless. The proliferation of content formats gives us options on how we opt to receive the information. Podcasts, videos, and audio books are all viable methods for accessing information. You must be literate, but you no longer have to be an avid reader.
What is important now is curiosity.
Do you have a desire to learn, are you dedicated to improvement? It's at your fingertips, customizable, contextual, inclusive, and boundless.

Nipsey Hussle said *"I steal advice. You don't have to tell me. I peep game in your demonstration. I'm a student of success"*. This is where the secondary market for information comes in, social media. The tidbits you can aggregate from TikTok, Instagram, Facebook. So often we see social media as a time succubus. It's all on how you use it. You're on your smart phone, you plugged in! Now you have to focus the curiosity. Focus on what helps you become what you want to be otherwise I'll be paraphrasing Mr. J Cole's love yours:

The good news my ni**a....you came a long way. The bad news my ni**a....you went the wrong way.

Reading ain't fundamental no more but knowledge is still power. Inside or outside IYKYK... could **show you where the red at where the blue at, where they flip that and where they bitch at let me put you on to game** (Game)! That's what knowledge is. HOV always shows how to move in a room full of vultures. Are you paying attention? Are you going past the lyrics and catchy flows to understand or you still just listening to rap? The breadcrumbs are there but if the curiosity isn't the result is nothing.

Learning isn't difficult BUT no one can do it for you. Your desire for greatness must be coupled with an insatiable curiosity and a hunger for knowledge. It's all there for the taking and now you have the tools.

CHAPTER 10
FINNA BE CONSEQUENCES AND REPERCUSSIONS

In season 1 of the Wire, Wallace asks youngin' **why can't you do the book problem right, if you're able to keep the count and the response is simple: If the count be wrong, they'll f**k you up.** The pain of messing up on the outside is immediate. The negative stimuli serve as motivation to stay on task and execute at a high level. Why isn't it as necessary to get the book problem right? Is it because there isn't a consequence for messing up in class? The desire to avoid physical pain is undeniable.

What we can't imagine, what we don't visualize or quantify is the agony of a slow painless demise. **Being broke at 30 give a ni**a the chills** (B.I.G.) when I heard that line it was the first time, I contemplated the price of not being successful. To understand the true cost of failing its imperative success is defined. Visualize what success looks like. Imagine how success feels. When that concept crystallizes mentally use it to define success.

Pain avoidance does not mean all is well. Assume average minimum wage in 2022 is $11.00. Working an average 40-hour week plus 10 hours of overtime every week puts you at $2,420 per month (let's pretend taxes don't exist) Is that sum worth 200 hours of life, 26% of a calendar month. Most worry about the pain of messing up the count. Think of the slow deliberate unrelenting grind of not solving the book problem. Failing to prioritize education formal or informal, has a price.

The cost is never achieving true potential.

Never realizing dreams. Never experiencing life. A fate worse than death.

Meek Mills Heaven or Hell lays it out perfectly

Some ni**as go to college.

Some ni**as go to jail

Some make it into heaven

Some make it into hell

Nobody wants to lose

Nobody wants to fail....

But some of us do fail. When the focus is solely on avoiding immediate stimuli that is deemed negative, often the future is sacrificed. So focused on surviving or enjoying the moment, the opportunity cost gets ignored. Every course of action has a consequence. Everyone has the power to shape their life.

Not having the vision to see the repercussion of choices can be costly.

CHAPTER 11
MOMMA AIN'T RAISE NO HOES

Outside the club doing the Bone Crusher rendition: *I ain't never scared! I AIN'T NEVER SCARED!* No matter how loud, no matter how many times you repeat it.... That's cap! You ain't never scared of what you know. It's safe, staying within familiar confines. Flourishing in an environment aligned with your preferences. Phrase it how you want but it's the familiarity and lull of the comfort zone.

It's easy to run to what's known, even when it's destructive. The false sense of bravado that comes from being anxious to display an idiotic affinity for known destruction is often accompanied by a catch phrase: I ain't no ho, I ain't no punk, I ain't no bitch, I ain't no... That philosophy is wanting. The million-dollar question is why not run to something you don't know? Run to something unexpected, something groundbreaking, something never seen, never done. Something with a result that is yet to be determined. True courage is to embrace the unknown not fulfilling the anticipated...

Be fearless. Aspire past what is expected. The expectations, assumptions, presumptions, and perceptions of others should not shape your vision or self-worth. No one can take your agency. Inside, outside, entrepreneurial, or corporate you have a vision for your life. Some will say they can't articulate it. Others rely on circumstance to define the path. That's not you. Nothing is going to happen to you. The key to it all is the realization that the accountability for your success is ultimately yours.

Every man has a right to decide his own destiny
(Bob Marley).

No special qualification is required.
No extraordinary background story is necessary.
You being you is more than enough.

You know what you want:

Have the courage to believe it. If it can't be formulated
in your head, how can you make it a reality?
The heart to say it (with your chest). Proclaim your vision.
The faith to expect it. Have complete trust in your ability
to materialize your vision.

The curiosity to investigate it. Ask the right questions.
Go past the initial answers. Figure out the how, the why
and the interconnectivity of all components.
The guts to go get it. The odds are irrelevant if it can
be done you can do it.

The self-respect to work diligently. People show up to work
consistently regardless of their mental or physical health.
Show up for yourself, no excuses.

Don't expect it to be easy.
Anything worth having requires effort.
Don't expect to be understood.
Very few have seen one like you.

The journey will be the most fulfilling part of the process.
It will be as rewarding as it will be difficult.
Your momma ain't raise no hoes.

You got this.

33

CHAPTER 12
WHO BRUNG YOU AND WHO YOU BROUGHT

"*And if you pattern my trend, I make you my protege*" (Nipsey Hussle). Mentors will not seek you out. Inside or outside, be patient, observe and follow the ebb and flow of your environment. Someone will always take notice of the apt pupil. Their interest doesn't dictate your protege status. Evaluate them as thoroughly as they evaluated you. Does their personal/ professional brand match your vision. Where they are; is that where you see yourself? A mentor may understand the game in theory, but ultimately, one can only teach what they know. They can only show you how to get where they are. Think of your mentor as a lease not a purchase. Of course, you can always purchase your lease but only if it's an ideal fit, as they grow, you grow. Dance with who brung you! It's a simple statement that holds weight. However, it does not mean you only have one dance partner.

The first part of that Nipsey rhyme: **"That's why they follow me huh? They think I know the way"**. As you progress through your grind (with the guidance of others) you'll begin nurturing those who "pattern your trend". To level up all forces must be harnessed. The efforts of mentors, to pull you up, your effort and the often forgotten, effort of peers and subordinates to push you up. These are the ones you brought. Your crew more than likely won't be on your level, but they'll see where you are heading and become invested in your success. Your job is to set the standard, be the example. Your sphere of influence will expand. Ironically, it's because you were smart enough to follow.

Never underestimate the power of relationships.

Regardless of where you stand in the mentor/mentee paradigm it's important you realize each role has responsibilities. The mentee is responsible for being an engaged student and an accurate representation of their mentor. It is also important that they serve as eyes and ears. You are closer to ground level and can offer insight not obvious from the higher levels. The mentor is responsible for the guidance and protection of their mentee, providing insight into navigating the slippery steps up the ladder of success. Wherever you stand act accordingly. Play your position skillfully and purposefully as they are essential to your overall success.

ACTION STEPS:

Identify who is in the position you see yourself in
Let them use you (chapter 4)
Identify who you can help
Teach them as much of the code as you can

There is a satisfaction and security that comes from working within a clique to achieve professional goals. Your clique isn't based on team assignments or projects. It's commonly referred to as the team within the team. Symbiotic relationships will always yield positive results. Be prepared to give as much as you take. The goal is to create an ecosystem that expands and strengthens all members.

You could go it alone but why?

LASTWORDS:
UP, UP, DOWN, DOWN, LEFT, RIGHT, LEFT, RIGHT, B, A, START

I don't know of an easy way to get to the bag. No short cut to glory or being successful. Along the path there will be trying moments, sad seasons, feelings of inadequacy or even worse imposter syndrome. How do you operate during these times? You use the only proven cheat code.

Have you ever heard of Pavlovian conditioning? If you haven't look up the experiment involving Pavlov's dogs.

CLIFF NOTES:

Ivan Petrovich Pavlov realized there was an association between events (sounds) and an animal's reaction as it pertained to producing saliva. When the dogs heard sounds associated with food they salivated. Even if there was no food.

Why is this important:

Dog, we can condition you as well. It's called Superhero Music (SM). An example of SM would be SIRIUS, known as the Chicago Bulls intro song from 1984 - 2004 (The Jordan Era). Sirius heralded the Michael Jordan Bulls.

This song accomplished 2 key things it inspired the Bulls players/fans and put fear in the hearts of their opponents.

ACTION STEPS:

Reflect on a time when you felt invincible.
Could have been a summer, a moment, or a whole year.
Everything was going right. You couldn't take an L if you tried.

What was the soundtrack to your season of invincibility?
When you identify that song play it 3 times in a row.
If it doesn't give you the feeling it's not the song.

Once the song is identified play it after your next
5 successful days.

For the next 21 days you'll play this song before you
begin to work (I suggest you never stop).

THE RESULT:

You've associated your SM with the mindset of being effective
and successful. Now when those feelings of inadequacy sneak
in take a moment, play your SM. Focus and envision your
success. Much like Pavlov's dogs you should begin to salivate.

This music reminds you of who you are. What you are capable
of. Most importantly you have been successful before.

Use your SM cheat code, as necessary.

YOUR THOUGHTS